This book has been

DISCARDED

By Freeport U.F.S.D

BAYVIEW AVENUE SCHOOL
FREEPORT, N.Y

BOOK # _____ 29715

D1173772

GREAT GRIZZLY WILDERNESS

A Story of the Pacific Rain Forest

by Audrey Fraggalosch

Illustrated by Donald G. Eberhart

Soundprints
Where Children Discover...

For my dear dad — A.F.

Dedicated in memory of my best friend Bill M. and to the loving support of my parents, Charles and Catherine E. — D.E.

Text copyright © 2000 Audrey Fraggalosch.
Book copyright © 2000 Soundprints, a division of Trudy Corporation,
353 Main Avenue, Norwalk, Connecticut.

Soundprints is a division of Trudy Corporation, Norwalk, Connecticut 06851.

All rights reserved. No part of this book may be reproduced or transmitted in any form or by any means whatsoever without prior written permission of the publisher.

Art Director: Diane Hinze Kanzler
Editor: Judy Gitenstein

First Edition 2000
10 9 8 7 6 5 4 3 2 1
Printed in Hong Kong

Acknowledgments:
   Our thanks to Dr. Charles Jonkel of The Great Bear Foundation, Missoula, Montana, for his curatorial review.
   Donald G. Eberhart would like to give special thanks to Deborah Watkins for her time and research efforts on his behalf.

Library of Congress Cataloging-in-Publication Data

Fraggalosch, Audrey.
     Great grizzly wilderness: a story of the Pacific rain forest / written by Audrey Fraggalosch; illustrated by Donald G. Eberhart. — 1st ed.
          p.   cm.
     Summary: A mother grizzly bear awakens from her hibernation and teaches her two cubs how to hunt and eat as much food as they can to prepare for next winter.
     ISBN 1-56899-838-4 (hardcover)   ISBN 1-56899-839-2 (pbk.)
     1. Grizzly bear — Juvenile fiction. [1. Grizzly bear — Fiction.   2. Bears — Fiction.]
I. Eberhart, Donald G., ill.   II. Title.
     PZ10.3.F837   Gr2000
     [Fic] — dc21
                                                                    99-044597
                                                                    CIP
                                                                    AC

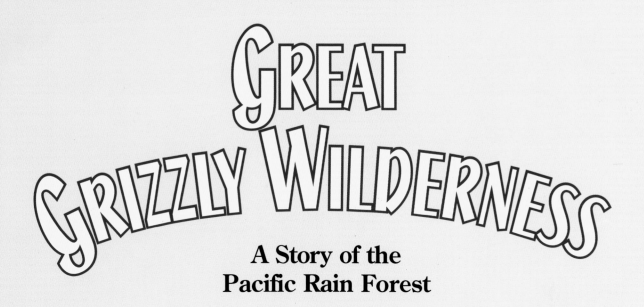

GREAT GRIZZLY WILDERNESS

A Story of the
Pacific Rain Forest

by Audrey Fraggalosch

Illustrated by Donald G. Eberhart

On a gray afternoon in January, a soft patter of misty rain falls on the Koeye River Valley along the northwest coast of British Columbia. Inside the dry, mossy hollow of a giant old cedar tree high on a mountain, a grizzly bear rolls over onto her back. Two tiny newborn cubs climb up on her warm, brown belly. They hum happily as they nurse on her rich milk. The mother bear gently licks her cubs before falling back into a deep sleep. The cubs snuggle and suckle close to their mother for the rest of the wet winter.

In April, the cubs follow their mother outside and down into the moist, green rain forest. Huge western hemlock, red cedar, and Sitka spruce trees, draped in mosses and lichens, tower above them.

The mother bear is hungry after sleeping all winter long. She searches for fresh grasses and the tender green shoots of young plants to eat. Sniffing the cool air, she catches the heavy scent of skunk cabbage and heads for its bright yellow flowers that glow like lanterns on the forest floor. The cubs tag along close behind her.

A loud, rapid hammering wakes the cubs from their nap near the skunk cabbage patch. In an old dead snag, a pileated woodpecker carves out a nest hole, whacking out wood chips with its powerful bill. Last year's cavity is now occupied by flying squirrels.

Nearby, a pair of ravens prepares to nest. To impress the female, the male raven tumbles and rolls in midair and then dives steeply to the ground. Both cubs run after the big black bird, but it takes off into the canopy to continue its courtship flight. Excited by the chase, the cubs tussle and tumble together on the soft, spongy mosses that carpet the forest floor like a fuzzy green blanket. The mother bear joins in the play. She runs after a cub and starts a game of tag.

Soon the cubs are big enough to follow their mother along well-worn trails through the rain forest where hundreds of generations of grizzly bears have walked before them. The mother bear steps in huge paw prints, some pressed almost a foot deep into the moss and mud. She lumbers past tall Sitka spruces, scarred by bear claws. High up on a wide, mossy branch, a marbled murrelet nests on a single egg.

Farther along the trail, a big male grizzly stands on his hind legs and rubs his back up and down against a tree. Some of his shedding fur catches in the bark. The mother bear quickly heads off to avoid this dangerous male who could attack her cubs.

When it is safe, the mother bear shows her cubs where to snack on salmonberries and the bright red berries of devil's club. A big banana slug chews holes in a two-foot-wide devil's club leaf. The cubs follow their mother down the trail to a beach. In the shallow waters, four river otters dip and dive for fish. Offshore, a small herd of northern sea lions rises out of the cold Pacific Ocean.

The mother bear stands up on her hind legs and sniffs the air. She smells wolf and deer droppings. She smells sedges and the sweetness of huckleberries. When she cannot smell another bear, she relaxes and tears up mouthfuls of the grass-like sedges. Still hungry, she leads her cubs to the beach to dig for clams and to look for crabs washed up by the tides.

Late in the summer, the mother bear senses it is time for the salmon to return to the river. She searches for a fishing spot where large overhanging branches keep the water cool enough for the salmon to spawn, or lay their eggs. Nearby, a tiny winter wren twitters and trills from its song perch in the thick understory.

With her cubs by her side, the mother bear patiently watches the bubbly surface of the water for telltale splashes. Suddenly, she charges into the river and chases a salmon around and around. Eventually, the mother bear grabs the wiggling fish in her mouth and brings it ashore. She pins it down with her large paws and bites into it. Streams of bright pink eggs squirt into the air. The cubs eagerly lick up the eggs.

Many other animals gather at the Koeye River. Orca whales follow migrating salmon up to the mouth of the river. Black-tailed deer drink from the shallow pools. Bald eagles swoop down from the treetops and carry away salmon in their long sharp talons to feed their young. Ravens, crows, and gulls patrol the shore looking for leftovers to eat. A rare white Kermode bear fishes up river, faraway from its larger cousins.

Some days as many as twenty-five grizzly bears fish the river. The biggest and strongest males get the best fishing spots, just below the waterfalls. The mother bear carefully chooses a place away from the dangerous males. The cubs wait on the bank and watch her every move. She wades into the water and swims with her head underwater, "snorkeling" for salmon.

When she comes up for air, the mother bear hears a high-pitched cry. One of her cubs is running as fast as it can away from a huge male grizzly. She rushes out of the water and charges full-speed after the dangerous male. She lashes out at him, raking his rear with her four-inch long claws. He whirls around, snarling at her. This gives the cub just enough time to pull itself up into a tree. The big male growls and snarls some more, but the cub is safe.

During the last weeks of summer and early fall, the bears eat as much as possible to fatten up for the long winter ahead. Sometimes the mother bear catches as many as ten salmon in an hour, and she may eat only the fattiest parts—the skin, brain, cheeks, and eggs.

When the big-leaf maples and alders shed their leaves and the heavy rains begin, the mother bear leads her cubs through the windswept forest and up the mountain, back to a winter den. They nibble on the last bearberries and bunchberries. Nearby, an elk chews on leaf-like lichens that have fallen from the canopy. In the branches above, a Douglas squirrel grabs a cone and then hides it underground for winter food. Higher up in the canopy, a hungry marten spies the squirrel, one of its favorite prey.

Inside the cavity of the den, the mother bear shows her cubs how to rake together a thick nest of mosses, lichens, and fallen leaves. The grizzly bears then curl up beside each other and fall asleep. Outside, a saw-whet owl hoots and fluffs its feathers to protect its small body from the cold and wet. In the distance, a pack of gray wolves lift their muzzles and howl their territorial claims over this part of the ancient rain forest. But the grizzly bears don't hear these songs. They sleep through the night and the next day and night—and for most of the winter without eating or drinking, seldom leaving their den.

In spring when the days grow longer,
the mother bear and her cubs slowly wake up
and stumble outside. Wisps of mist float overhead
as the bears wander among the tall, curling sword
ferns licking up raindrops. Sunlight filters through
the canopy and highlights an opening in the rain
forest where a tree fell during last winter's storms.
It is now a nurse log for young trees. Under the
moss-covered log, a long-toed salamander looks
for insects to eat. A rufous hummingbird buzzes
by. It has flown thousands of miles from its
wintering grounds in Mexico to nest in the rain
forest and stops to drink nectar from a pink
salmonberry flower. The bears are hungry too
after not eating for so many months.

The mother bear leads her cubs down to the mouth of the Koeye River to feast on fresh green sedges. She spends hours digging up the nutritious roots of the rice root lily with her powerful paws. The cubs will remember where and when to find these plants next spring. This summer they will learn how to fish and by next year or the year after they will be ready to live on their own. And so the ancient cycle of the great bear family continues as it has for thousands of years in the Pacific rain forest.

The Pacific Rain Forest

The Pacific rain forest, also known as the temperate rain forest, extends from Alaska south into British Columbia, Washington, Oregon, and northern California. It is a lush coniferous forest that dates back to the time when dinosaurs walked the earth. The Pacific rain forest provides habitat for thousands of birds, mammals, and insects, many of which live high up in the canopy. It is also home to endangered or threatened species, such as the grizzly bear.

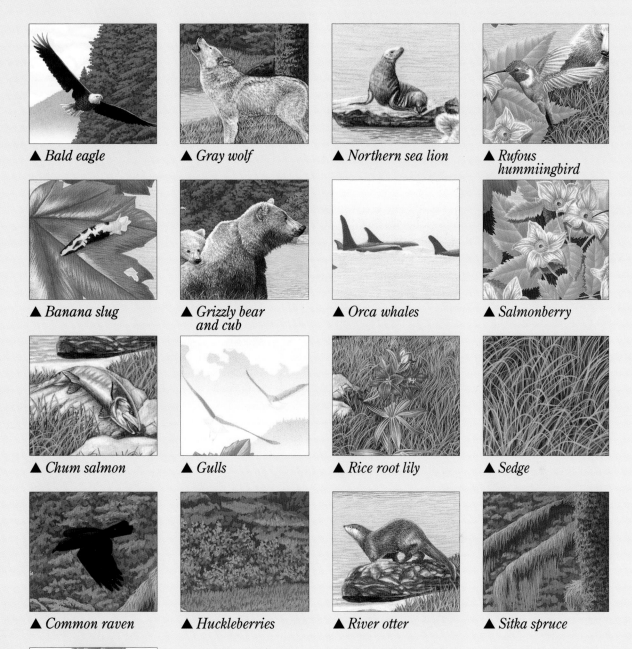

▲ Bald eagle

▲ Gray wolf

▲ Northern sea lion

▲ Rufous hummiingbird

▲ Banana slug

▲ Grizzly bear and cub

▲ Orca whales

▲ Salmonberry

▲ Chum salmon

▲ Gulls

▲ Rice root lily

▲ Sedge

▲ Common raven

▲ Huckleberries

▲ River otter

▲ Sitka spruce

▲ Devil's club

F   29715
Fra
     Fraggalosch, Audrey
     GREAT GRIZZLY
     WILDERNESS...